A
CROOKED
FINGER
BECKONS

L. Patrick Carroll

PEANUT BUTTER PUBLISHING

Seattle, Washington
Portland, Oregon
Denver, Colorado
Vancouver, B.C.
Scottsdale, Arizona
Minneapolis, Minnesota

Peanut Butter Publishing
2207 Fairview Avenue East, Houseboat Number Four
Seattle, Washington 98102
(206) 860-4900

Table of Contents

Divine Eyes Never Close

Prelude To Poetry

Unlike more gifted poets do I see.
No daring metaphors dance from my tongue.
Rare lofty simile leafs this simple tree.
But I have language loved since I was young.

In awe of words, I write of grace, and hope,
Of people I have cherished, dreams fulfilled,
Or dashed against life's rocks. My constant scope,
The cross, yet more — for all that's momentarily killed
Can rise. I sing a song of life, along —
Side death, of ashes overcome, of all
That if it does not end us makes us strong . . .
I praise each fragile rising, from each fall.

These poems, if poems they be, receive.
Word gifts of everything I dare believe.

Preface

I have always heard, indeed, have always taught, that a poem or any other work of art should stand on its own; the biography of the artist is extraneous to the work. As years go by I no longer believe that to be true. Milton's blindness deeply altered his art. Oscar Wilde's sexual orientation colors every word he wrote. Gerard Manly Hopkins' conversion to Catholicism, his Jesuit vocation to find God in all things, his abiding sense of personal failure all weave their way into every ounce of his marvelous poetry. Ignorance about the facts of an artist's life means we only have access to a small percentage of the depth and scope of the art itself.

So, I preface these poems with some small biographical data.

Raised a Catholic by deeply Catholic parents in an almost entirely Catholic neighborhood, I entered a Jesuit Seminary at eighteen in 1954. I was a Jesuit for forty-four years, a priest for thirty-one of those. As a Jesuit I taught and/or administered schools, was a parish pastor for many years, was by all accounts an excellent liturgist and preacher. I directed numerous retreats and wrote six books on various areas of spirituality. I loved the Society of Jesus, and, for the most part, loved being a priest. To all outward appearances I was successful at both.

In 1995 at the age of sixty-one, everything began to noticeably disintegrate. My health began to fail, and after a cardiac arrest I no longer had the energy for the task. I lost my taste for the ministry and everything became, simply, hard work.

Most of these poems were spawned during the period

of transition from Jesuit priest to married layman, at an age when most are simply moving slowly into retirement. I experienced all that I had known as broken. I trusted God to help me begin again. God has, and I did.

Having written books before, I found myself no longer drawn to longer pieces and began to try to capture in a few words the experiences I was having; began to put on paper what otherwise seemed likely to crush my fragile heart. I wrote about my pain and new beginnings, wrote to my now-wife, wrote about family and friends in their wrestling with life, wrote about the people and place of Providence Vincent House where I now work — a simple apartment building for the elderly and/or disabled poor.

Many of these poems were written for the people in my life.

A Wedding Vow was written to my wife, Dee, before our wedding and was recited at the ceremony. *Diana, Dee* was written to her as well, for her birthday, the year before we were married.

I wrote *A Mother's Hope* when I was very young and I was surprised to rediscover it just a year or two ago. Over the years I wrote very little poetry. Still I recall having a sense of vast enjoyment when I did so. This very early piece speaks perhaps of promise. I wrote the poem as an assignment while in the Seminary where each Sunday morning we had "*scriptio*," a period of writing. These Sunday morning exercises held no expectation of real art, just a growing ability to put pen to paper (literally in those days, I might add). I have only the vaguest recollection of the poem because my mother died on Mother's Day, that May, in 1958. I do not know whether, in her long illness, she even had a chance to read the poem. I trust in her awareness of it now, from wherever mother's go when their task is finished.

In 1943, my mother sat by my side for a year as I recovered from polio. She watched me grow up, delighted at and, I suspect, sometimes fearful of my normalcy. She stood lovingly by as I wrecked the family car several times, loved beer, did not study, and then, she wept, but supported me when I left home to enter the Jesuit Seminary in Sheridan, Oregon, in 1954. Beloved Zelda died when I was only 22-years-old before I ever got the chance to know her as an adult. I was delighted when my brother discovered this 45-year-old piece which I find delightful in its youthful enthusiasm, self-deprecation and parental fondness.

I am fortunate, however, to have a second mother. My father married Edith Jacobson in 1962. Now, in 2002, she has been my mother for forty years . . . longer than either my first mother, or my father. Edith has loved me through thick and thin. She has relied on me, advised me, comforted and supported me as she has all in our family. She is a woman of wit and wisdom, grace and humor. For Edith's 86th birthday, I wrote *Eighty-Six Januaries*. Now, as she nears ninety, the poem seems more true, more poignant, than it did just four years ago.

Millennial Anniversary was written for my brother John and his wife Judy who have been married at this writing for 47 years. We celebrated this wedding anniversary during the millennium while I went though personal changes in my entire life and while their sons were going through divorces, quite painfully. John and Judy's commitment was an island of sanity in a sea of madness. Pam and Paul Schell also celebrated an anniversary at the same time — so the poem was two-fold.

Turning Twenty-One was written for my step-son, Morgan Dowe Davidson.

TallyAnn Turns Forty is for a niece I cherish.

Love's Dance Begins was written for the wedding of Kirsten Mello, my niece. It could be for almost any wedding, however; the beginnings of love before reality has reared any head at all!

Away with Words was written in honor of Colby Chester, a friend, poet, teacher, and actor; a master of words, wired, an honest expert on many things. I am grateful for his gift of language, and, like many things, his blessing can be his curse.

For John, The One Jesus Loved was written for my lifetime friend John Leonard. It was composed for his retirement from the ministry of teaching after 30 years, a ministry preceded by 18 years in the Society of Jesus. John has experienced painful moments, loss, personal failure, but rises above them with an almost unparalleled grace and charm.

Four Score and Fourteen was written to honor my friend Joe Diamond.

For Sally was written for Sally Martin, who died on her birthday at 101-years-old.

Several of these poems were written for or inspired by people I met through my work at Vincent House and other places at which I've been honored to serve. *To Ken* was written about Ken Young, a tenant at Vincent House who lived on oxygen. He was a former "street drunk" who mellowed in his later years, warm, fighting for each breath, grateful for every favor . . . a hard exterior, but marshmallow within. *Farewell to Florence* was written for the memorial service of Florence, a long time tenant at Vincent House. Each day she walked 4 blocks for lunch, blind and deaf, through the crowded Pike Place Market; fed the local birds each day, came each morning for a cup of communal coffee, unable to see the milk and sugar she inevitably spilled — a treasured presence in our halls and in my life. *Old Along with Me* was written for the memorial service of Ed Hathaway, a wonderful 80-year-old tenant, a double amputee who lived on the streets for years, but in his later years had taken to reading a book a day and listening to symphonies. He suffered continually, but refused to be mastered by pain. *Broadway Bill* is a prose piece for Bill Downey who was at the very center of every liturgical or social event at St. Leo's for all of my years there.

In 1977-8, Holy Names Sister, Katherine Dyckman, S.N.J.M., and I gave retreats and trained native retreat directors in the small country of Lesotho, in Southern Africa. Four poems from that year are included. The first, *Stormed Memory*, describes my reactions to a violent thunder storm in this otherwise dry, mountainous land; the second, *Lesotho*, more my personal reaction to that country. Some reflections before a prayer workshop, *To A Contemplative Anglican Sister*, speaks for itself. *Beatitude* tries to capture the emotional experience of having an extremely poor Basotho man return a lost wallet to me, containing about $300 on a day when I had just preached about the Beatitude's — Blessed/happy are the Poor in Spirit! Finally, *Surprise*, describes my delight at having a wonderful African Sister visit my mother in San Francisco — a visit both cherished, as did I.

Other poems are more personal in nature, related to my years in the priesthood and my decision to leave. *Who Am I Now*, for instance, was written the day I left the Society of Jesus after 42 years; wrestling, as a symbol, with my name, within, my identity. *Ready and Willing* was composed for the 32nd anniversary of my ordination. This poem really came the summer after I had left the active ministry — an anniversary outside the box. *Reluctant Surrender* is based upon The Suscipe ("Take, Receive") which is a familiar Jesuit prayer inviting God to take everything; it was all a gift to begin with; a prayer of surrender to God's love and care. It's a prayer I said myriad times as a Jesuit, but only understood once I had departed.

No Branch Grows Alone, written in 1966, a year before Ordination to the priesthood reflects my dawning realization, perhaps for the first time, how important human love was even in the life of one vowed to celibacy.

Christology From Below is the results of encountering contemporary biblical studies, especially regarding Jesus — initially disillusioning, but finally, illuminating.

No Comedy is a poetic counter-part to a longer work, *Chaos or Creation*, about the Mid-life transition. *"Blessed are They Who Mourn,"* flows out of a parish's Lenten prayer experience during the Gulf War as we prepared for Easter.

Having experienced a Cardiac Arrest, and attendant heart problems in July of 1995, I did not expect to celebrate Christmas that year. I did, and *Birth Happens* resulted . . . a rather dark, Christmas poem. Other Christmases; other poems.

For many years I struggled, mostly with success, but also with noticeable failure, to love broadly, widely, many, many people in many, many places. I stove to mirror God's ubiquitous love. Now I experience my life as a call to love quite individually, quite specifically, a few people where I work, a handful of friends, my faithful family, and one woman, my wife, Dee. This task is just as daunting.

Friends have encouraged me to collect into a single volume poems I have written over the years. I postponed doing so because I doubted they possessed any universal or even general interest. Most seem solipsistic, self-centered, or, at the very least grounded in people and events most personal to me. Still, Emerson somewhere asserted that if one can capture anything true about his or her experience such a writer will, at the same time, capture something common to the human spirit, for we are all united in some kind of "over soul."

In that spirit, without apology, I offer these poems; my poems, my life, my fears, pain, joys, and inspirations. If my experience helps you understand or even cherish similar experiences of your own, I will be grateful . . . and perhaps, so will you.

That's Why They
Told the Story

Act of Faith

It has something to do with Jesus —
This cross,
manufactured by my own mistakes.

Somewhere,
beneath the raw,
        life-changing
unimagined,
yet, always under everything, feared,
pain:

Jesus,
with crooked finger, beckons,
"Come."

Birth Happens

Fresh out of hope,
Expectations dimmed by darkness
Of age and illness,
Weary of an inner/outer world, gone mad . . .
When, despite the bumper stickers
"Birth happens!"

Heart starts again,
Blood pumps through brain and body,
Spirit stirred by stable full of promise,
"Birth happens!"

The Jesus story, told again,
Denies my darkness,
Will not let me fold my tent
When love is pitched beside it.
In me, and around,
"Birth happens!"

So, I will live while life endures,
And love as best I can,
And tell the Jesus story
To myself, and you.
The story starts each time
"Birth happens!"

"Merry Christmas"
From an Easter point of view,
From one, if not exactly risen from the dead,
Still close enough to say,
"Birth happens!"

Christmas Eve

Bright, unwanted, winter sun,
No jingling bells —
Nothing in the air,
Nor inner breath says,
"Christmas."

Changes of another year
Their dreadful toll taken
From myriad booths anonymous,
leave but small change behind.

God's birth,
Believed this Eve,
A choice against
Both gut and mind's find grain.

Sometimes . . .
Now —
Faith,
As if an uphill climb
In mountain air,
Gasping for breath,
Gets none.

Still, in unfelt, breathless
Winter Creed,
God is born again,
Needed if
Scarcely noticed,
Till Easter's flowers spring.

Christmas Gift

Divinity reclining,
Resting, after sweaty birth
in hay.
Humanity erect — First time potent
Since the tree, the apple
And the "no."

Divinity saying "yes"
To all we are,
Runny noses,
Stomach ache
And all.

Humanity fumbling
To affirm
All God is said to be —
Wise, Just,
And, purely,
Love.

God taking on
Our struggle,
We assuming,
Majesty.

Divine emptied of
Everything,
The human heart
Receiving more than
Wildly imagined.

God gives,
We get,
Who wins?

Matter Over Mind

A *Christmas Poem*

Yes, I've read the books that tell "The Truth."
Perhaps two paragraphs are all we know of him,
If knowledge comes in fact, through fact,
and texts redacted.
There may have been no virgin birth,
no star, no crowded inn, nor angels in the night.
That song may silent be.

We know a man named Yesu lived and died,
and some say lived again, lives still.
We know he spoke in parables,
threw rocks at hallowed, glass encased traditions,
shared meals ritually with friends who followed him.
We know he called the Jewish God (unspoken Yahweh)
Father.

That's all!
Yet much to know of God.

For if he lived, then born surely,
birth in every case miraculous.
The mystery is not less repeated.

The myths with which we spin the story are not
    less true
than all the wonders that arise in lives
of those who shape their dreams upon them.

We judge a tale by the tears or peace it bears.
We judge a symphony by cords it touches in
    our guts.
We judge poem or picture by response that swells
through flesh and blood, enlivening.

The human spirit springs from truth
buried deep beneath what mind, meticulous,
can measure or distill.

So, still,
the star shines bright
above a manger's child.
A man and woman meditate mystery
they no more understand than any parents ever did.

The promise that resides within that child
still fosters faith, hurls hope, leaps love;

The wisest of us wander still to search him out.

Easter

It's not about Jesus —
What happened to him after death —
but me,
And you —
What happens to us
Because of Jesus.

That's why
They told the story,
In the beginning,
Stopping strangers,
Grabbing lapels;
Left home and hearth
For jail,
Sometimes death.
Couldn't cease shouting
Because it changed them.

Not most about what happens after death,
But how, why, whether,
We live now.

Easter says —
Celebrates —
Out of the worst
Comes the best —
Night to day,
Dis-ease to ease,
Pain to promise,
Defeat to dance,
Yes,
Cross to crown.

Not in some heaven,
Distant, only —
Rather, now,
Right here.

This our Easter
Alleluia
Song.

Love's Dance Begins
A Wedding Poem

First Movement of a Dance,
Before the awkwardness sets in
With complex steps, as music moves
Beyond first stanza and refrain.

First moments of a game,
When victory seems assured;
Hope high,
Before that first deflating fumble.

Initial burst of Faith,
When God of Love seems evident,
Before the cross brings doubt,
Before inevitable dark descends.

First blush of Love,
Fresh as Spring,
Too often just as fleeting.

We celebrate such new beginnings,
Entrusting you into tomorrow,
Believing you will dance still
When music stops awhile.
Re-group, rise up, go on
Despite each painful pause
On Calvary's climb.

We, Winter people, trust
Your nascent love
To find its way
Through heat of Summer suns,
And passions' pull,
Survive dead leaves
of Autumn,
Winter's woes and winds,
To reach beyond each season's
Challenge to your love,
Until you live together,
Spring again.

Millennial Anniversary

In a world of broken promises,
With razors, diapers, income
    all disposable —

When life is mostly measured
    by inches or millennia,
    but almost never
Day-in, day-out, forever —

When free agency pervades,
    franchise stars are expendable,
    nothing lasts,
    everything changes, passes away,
dies out —

When planned obsolescence
    profit promises —

While even close around you
Loved ones,
    despite their fondest hopes,
    and fervent struggles,
May not manage life,
    or let love last,
    As we had hoped —

You two stand,
Together,
Cry, together,
Celebrate, together
Go on, together
Into whatever future holds —

While we who love you
Clap,
Rejoicing, in the gift you are
        To us,
        To one another,
And to our otherwise
So fragile
World.

A Wedding Vow

Though wordsmith self-proclaimed,
I'm mostly mute
This wedding day.

Words of hope,
Fidelity's expressions,
Love's language —
All used up,
Exhausted.

I long to tell you,
In ways you can savor,
Trust, and build a life on . . .
No new words come,
A faucet without water,
A light bulb dimmed by use.

So,
Old words heard before
You hear again:
"Forever . . ."
"Good times and bad . . ."
"Honor . . ."
"Cherish . . ."
"I do."

Without apology
I mouth the trite and true,
Promising that
Years from now,
When I have smithed,
With every ounce of life I have,
These ancient words,
They'll come to mean
More than they've meant to you,
Or anyone,
Till now!

On an Anniversary

I had not known before, such love . . . not this,
where everyday the same face first is seen,
where evening ends and morning starts with kiss
profound, though sometimes strange, forgotten
by neglect. Had not known arm and leg
and heart entwined so close, so fragile too,
that every word, each phrase, all thought must beg
for patience, understanding, empathy anew.

I never knew what daily love required,
nor its rewards, nor ever hoped to know,
till I wed you, and then most deep desired
into that knowledge desperately to grow.

So, though I know not yet all love-life's rule,
still, these have been two wondrous years of school.

Christmas in Afghanistan

He did not come
Powerful into that land
Where Roman power
(not Palestinian,
Even then without a land)
Ravaged his people,
Retaliation harshly crucified.

Did not come
Rich into a world of hunger,
Where their scarcity
More than our greed
Kept bellies swollen.

Was not born, his mother
Monitored, kept safe,
(Even just a day
as some Insurance policy proclaimed)
But in a cave,
Like those on CNN
Each desert day,
Where terrorists
(Children and women, too)
Huddle from our bombs.

Born not in a city grand,
No New York,
Even with towers tumbled,
Nor (disputed even then)
Jerusalem.
Rather a town, on maps unnoticed
Until some battle rages,
Or God is born.

Though royal his lineage
His parents had no fear
Some "death tax," would
Inheritance deplete;
A laborer (without a union's)
Son.

Emmanuel arrived,
God with us,
Sharing broken pieces
Our passion and our pain.

Hopes too —
Of lions lying down with lambs,
Valleys smoothed, hills leveled,
Bombs, land mines, hearts disarmed;
Shared dreams
Of differences denied,
No Jew or Greek,
No man or woman, slave or free,
No Christian, Muslim, Jew or Buddhist,
No us, no them.

Thus came he to a wounded world,
Not much different then from now.
Our world, those broken pieces,
That passion and that pain
Crushed him,
Dead.

Should he be still alive
As we, however haltingly, espouse,
So be his hopes and dreams

Creating Hell
or Home

Vincent House

Above the Market,
At the marvelous urban bottom
A pale green home for a city's
Anonymous dwellers.

Behind plastered walls
Sixty stories go on.

Though fully woven some already seem,
Yarns continue to spin —
A bottle left behind,
A victory over death, if only for today,
A quilt or question finished,
A tie tied by palsied hands,
A light bulb shines anew in darkness,
A plugged toilet flushes once again,
A bath taken,
A smoke shared outdoors in the wind.

One ancient sweeps the walkway,
Another, younger, simply sits
Relaxed,
Compulsed no longer.

Here amidst the smells of Sound,
Fish, Hops —
Sometimes, excrement —
Life compresses to a center
Simply seen.

Grateful the lucky few
Sensing the mystery
of Incarnation.

Reality Check

Never Together
Except by chance,
Or Whimsical Divine Design,
But together here we be,
Ruddy cheek by aged jowl.

Whether happily,
Oblivious to place,
Or curious
Over which forgotten sin
Merited this
Peculiar punishment,
By stroke, or stroke of luck,
From someone's aid or AIDS,
Blown by ill wind,
Ill health,
Or best breeze,
Together

Now — the trick —
Creating hell or home.

After Six Months
at Vincent House

Faces, stories too, familiar now.
  Familiarity breeding,
    Surely not,
    contempt,
But compassion, fondness,
  Laughter, admiration,
Hope.

Compassion as in
"suffering with,"
infirmity, fragility,
empty pockets,
dashed dreams,
best years apparently behind.

Fondness — heart strings daily strummed
by that story or this,
Teasing easily love
from wounded heart.

Laughter at our foibles —
keys down the trash bin,
Request for friggin Easter basket,
endless talking
to one who cannot hear,
a slightly tilted cake.

Unbounded *admiration* of those
Whose each day rising seems an act of courage.

All hurling *hope*,
The expectation confident
that tomorrow will be
Even better than today — and today
Was Wonderful!

Old Along with Me

Not for Sissies,
This Aging.
Things do fall apart,
No center holds,
Sight narrows,
Haunches broaden,
Legs stumble,
Hands shake,
Fragility's head rears
Everywhere.

Is this some second birth?
These aches, birth pangs?
Is life somehow
not departing only
But coming too?

Is there ahead
Some precious insight
taking place of sight;
some vision broadening
as well as hips;
Some rising in these falls;
Some stability not shaken
No matter how hands tremble?

Will these wheel chairs
Evolve into our thrones
as lame dance,
blind see,
and in our poverty
of heart and mind and spirit,
we hear,
finally, and forever,
Good News?

Providence

To see
ahead of time, or trouble;
apparently, to care
about what's seen.
If not to stop
at least to
offer opportunity
to duck.

No puppet master
Pulling strings to ease
Our imbecilities,
Or chance disasters.
Tragedy will still occur —
Darkness deservedly or no —
But, suddenly,
A friend appears to walk beside us,
A phone call,
random meeting,
or letter
lights a path,
Rainbow, song, or sunset,
Something unforeseen
by any but this
Providence
hurls hope.

Who see the world in this light
will name this
Sight —
ahead of time,
so providential —
God!

Vincent House Spring

To a courtyard,
Surrounded by simplicity,
Comes Autumn
Everywhere,
Painting beauty,
Outside once darkened doors —
Red, yellow, splash of green,
A hint of heaven past change.

Colors crash, where before
Only pallor —
More loveliness than ever,
At year's end —
Dying strangely beautiful
When God's fingers touch,
Transform,
And promise life
In some new, inevitable
Spring.

To Ken

Slumped in his chair, each breath a war, with wounds
From battles over years ago, we hear
His weariness unmasked. A fragile fear
Assails this once strong frame, the rattling sounds
Of death not far away. He barks both for,
And at the help he's given. Resenting, from
His loneliness, that love will dare to come,
where none or little has been known before.

"Farewell, oh thick-skinned friend," our final song.
We wheel him through the door, afraid this sight
The last we shall enjoy of one who's known our night,
Our day, our table, and our heart. "So long."

We pause in deference to life's fickle span.

Farewell to Florence

No longer gulls
Gathered at our door,
Hoping for their hungers to be fed,
Uniquely, with her manna.

No longer tourists,
Like a Red Sea,
Parting on the market's streets,
The chariot,
Her walker,
Leading to the promised land
of a free lunch.

No more mornings
Italicized by her,
Waiting at our common door,
Her cup to fill.
No longer creamer,
Victim of her sightless eyes,
Abundant on our floor.

No longer gratitude
Expressed for smallest favor,
Coffee re-fill,
Elevator door held open,
Word of welcome
Falling on deaf ears.

All passed away
With her.

Despite apparent ease
With which
Such rituals,
Ephemeral,
Have gone,
We mourn.

This Man,
This Gift

Turning Twenty-One

Like Abraham,
Too old to have a child,
Much less a child so old!
Yet, from my wife's loins,
Into my life,
Springs this giant man,
Enveloping, more than shaking,
My hand,
Filling, beyond entering,
My life,
Inviting, not only opening
My heart.

I wish I knew him small,
Would wish a part of forming
His past as well as future,
Wish years already passed
Lay yet before us both.
Vain hope.

Still,
I can and do give all but infinite thanks
That after barren years
I welcome warmly
Whatever years we have ahead.

Now twenty-one
I will only ever know,
A step beyond my child,
This man, this gift,
This son.

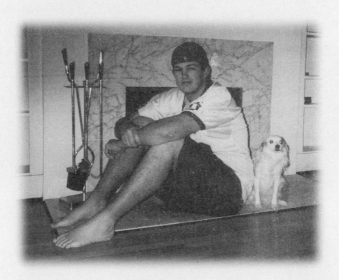

Away with Words

For three-score years
He's had his way with them.
Held them in his fingers,
Slid them off a gilded tongue;
Unfolded, sold, cajoled,
Poems, cars, friend and foe.

Words have been his fist
For fighting,
His wand, for wooing,
His justice sword and shield.

Eloquent,
He's spoken tomes
Of words, words, words,
To anyone who'd hear,
Of nature's plight,
A wounded world,
A poor man's dreams,
A drama's denouement,
Or auto's ambience.

Even to the deaf,
(Or those who wish they were)
He's spoken words
Beyond belief.

Now, aging,
Before life's mystery,
Love's demands,
Earth's fragility,
Perhaps a silence,
Comfortable,
Still more eloquent,
Can finally come.

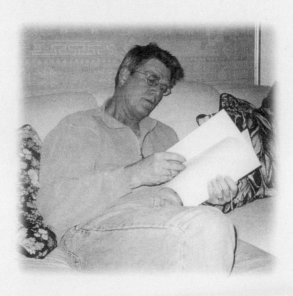

A Mother's Hope

You brought me forth from God knows where,
Still lacking teeth and wanting hair,
With gurgling gibberish in my talk
Full thirteen months till I could walk.
No infant tears bedewed my eyes,
I shook the halls with screams and cries.
"This child has promise," you yet declared,
But let's behold how I have fared.

At five-years-old, in tattered clothes
I found unwarranted repose
And slept beneath my brother's bat —
Upon home plate, he'd knocked me flat.
As, once again, sans teeth I lay,
Quite horrified, you look and say:
"This boy will one day win a name,
Despite his slender, toothless frame."

Again, at eight, I'm nigh to death
And anxiously beneath your breath
You say: "If life remains he'll be
The pride of millions, wait and see."
And live I did, through your hard work
And nature's unexplained quirk.
Again, proclaiming future worth,
You say, "Someday he'll rock the earth."

A few months later, John again
Became the cause of mutual pain,
A plaster gun my lips did part
To break my tooth, your loving heart.
Yet beauty lacking from my face
Did you desert me in disgrace?
Ah no, fond mother yet foretold
That I'd grow famous, growing old.

Recall the night I took the car
Around the block, "I won't go far."
Despite my tenderness of years
I verified your greatest fears —
A tiny dent, a year too soon,
Befell your blundering buffoon.
Yet you forgave again; you said:
"He'll be something before he's dead!"

And as my school days crept by
These wrecks recurrent multiply.
But fractured fenders you forgave
Each time I promised to behave.
The nights my angel drove me home
'Cause hops controlled by hazy dome,
You looked beyond my present state
And still insisted I'd be great!

And as I write these words in rhyme,
Reflecting my mis-spent lifetime,
I see no real cause for hope,
That I'll be president or Pope,
Yet still you say success I'll find
To honor you and human kind.
And, mother dear, if this comes true,
God knows I'll owe it all to you!

Four Score and Fourteen
A *Birthday Poem for Joe Diamond*

Scarcely imaginable,
Such span of years,
Changes wondrous in the world dreamt,
Doubtless death, destruction,
Lost opportunities,
Life's unavoided darkness,
Laughter, love,
Projects possible,
then realized . . .
Life's Light!

How awesome to remember,
Savor, be thankful,
For these many days,
The faces come and gone,
And those still here.

We who honor you,
Marvel, not at longevity alone,
But bow before the grace
The dignity, the honest care,
Accompanying each moment.

We celebrate your life lived well,
Grateful to have touched a bit of it,
Hopeful, (despite odds)
For many more,
With us.

Eighty-Six Januaries
To Edith

Eighty-six Januaries
With all the dark uncertainty
that winter brings,

Eighty-six rotations of the seasons
bringing
blossoms from dead branches,
light from dark,
life from death,
Hope.

Eighty-six cycles
you have watched for us
how sudden tragedy,
or slow, relentless sufferings
and every human hurt
is survivable.

Eighty-six times
after Winter,
you have stood up again,
embraced with love
the fragile world
we inhabit
together,
and urged us all to Spring.

For John,
The One Jesus Loved

So many years,
Speaking a word,
Deeply believed,
Sometimes cruelly cracked,
But never broken.

Years of overflowing,
Contagious laughter,
Ironies enjoyed,
Incongruities celebrated,
Perhaps
Masking tears too deep to flow.

Classroom years,
Fostering faith,
Hurling hope
Teaching people,
Young and old alike —
never at your feet, but —
by your side.

Years struggling
to believe
That love from you
ever was enough
Or for you
ever earned.

You've aimed so high,
Sometimes fallen far, and fast,
Wanted so much to give,
Yet held much back,
With eloquence you've spoken
Of freely given grace —
Though doubting you deserve.

Finally,
(like John whose name you bear)
You come this night
Surrounded by us all
(Others elsewhere,
Too numerous to name)
Those befriended,
Taught,
Nourished,
Cherished —
Affirming
(what you've always
Hoped, more than anything,
to know . . .)
You, John,
The disciple Jesus loved!

For Sally
A 100th Birthday Poem

We have known
The chapters at the back,
The denouement.
We guess the Preface,
The inciting incidents.

The tale of your life
Is not mystery,
But Romance.

We saw the lines of love
Etched in your brow,
Smiling in your eyes.

You are an Easter story.
There will be no end.

Broadway Bill

"Celebrate Life" . . .
I have learned how to cel-
ebrate from people with
handicapping conditions who
are so central to our parish
community. One of these
people was Bill, (whom we
lovingly called Broadway
Bill) who once led a sophisti-
cated cynical doctor to a simple faith. Bill often led
us in prayer, in dance, in celebration.

I remember most vividly a Holy Spirit mass some
years ago; I think this constitutes the liturgical high-
light of my life . . .

St. Leo Parish community begins our year togeth-
er, as many schools do, with a renewal of Spirit early
in September. We re-create the Spirit of Pentecost
as best we can. This liturgy has become one of our
major celebrations. This particular Spirit mass
ended with a small parade. A woman dressed as a
clown came into the church after communion. To
the melody of our parish theme song about the
Raggedy Band, she wandered through the church
inviting children (and others brave enough) to join
her. She passed out kazoos and drums and bells and
bottles to bang on. About thirty children joined in
her parade. Bill also joined in, bringing up the rear
of the parade as it wove throughout the community.
The clown had timed her march to have the children
come to lay down their instruments before the altar

as the final verse ended; then they would disperse back to their places.

All went well, except that Bill was not yet done parading. All the others had returned to their places, but as we sang the final words, Bill did one more trip down the center aisle, grinning from ear to ear, ringing his bell and dancing. We sang:

And did you know
That the lead child walking doesn't want to go?
And can you see
Where Broadway turns into Calvary?
Boom ticka, ticka, ticka
Boom ticka, ticka, ticka
Boom ticka, ticka ticka boom."

Bill returned to the altar alone, gently laying down his bell at the altar as the last note sounded. He turned solemnly to the congregation and with impeccable timing, bowed. We applauded. He bowed again, and then again.

A responsible adult was just getting out of her pew to retrieve Bill, but he knew his moment was over and went to the foot of the altar platform, turned, and bowed his head to await the final prayer which he knew to be next.

Several minutes later, through my tears, I prayed the final prayer for God's spirit, but already the Spirit was in our midst. Bill, unfettered by the customs or conditions that bind the rest of us had unleashed that Spirit in us and I thank God we had sense enough not to hamper him. We were led to God, like the cynical doctor, by the apparently weakest among us.

Mimi's Birthday Poem

First seen from distance,
Idealistic, Vanier spirited,
Knowing very young
We all are wounded.

Admired
For the care of many,
Then of one,
Cassandra,
Uneasily loved,
With less than gratitude.

Known from afar
As teacher,
Woman of faith,
Embracing those outside
straight rows,
Whose pencils,
Hearts, spirits,
(perhaps broken)
Could be sharpened
By the blades of love
Unfeigned and free.

Then,
Heard of only,
Fondly,
By the friends we shared.

In the latter stages
of your now half-century
of Life, grace-filled,
Known
(I'm proud to say)
As friend.

I give both God
And you,
Much Thanks

How Suffering Saves
In Memory of Madalin Douglass 1904-2001

On Friday, Madalin Douglass died, just a few
days short of her ninety-seventh birthday. Madalin
taught me more than any one else about God; and
specifically about God's love and about how suffer-
ing, somehow, satisfies that love. Jesus' redemptive
death — a death that pleases God — is still a mys-
tery, but at least, the mystery now has analogous
handles I can grasp.

The most difficult thing to understand about the
Christian faith is, perhaps, how the suffering of Jesus
accomplishes our redemption. How is God satisfied
by Jesus' death on the cross? Put more boldly, what
kind of God wants his son to suffer? More than one
person has turned away from the God of Jesus
because the religion seems to be built on a sadistic
parent to whom a son's suffering and death — the
most painful imaginable — somehow ends this
Father's anger at his children, and ushers in a new
age built upon this symbol of the cross.

I wrestled with this challenge all my adult life. I
could not understand how the death of Jesus *redeems* us.

Then I met Madalin.

Let me step back a moment, then return to the
awesome lesson Madalin taught.

Madalin herself is not well known, though she
deserves to be. Her son, Jim Douglass, is much more
famous. Jim, with his wife Shelley, is one of the true
saints of our era. As a theologian, Jim helped influ-
ence the Vatican II statement on the questionable

morality of nuclear weapons, and has written several
books on the Christian invitation to non-violence. I
think especially of *Lightening from East to West.* Jim
was the primary intellectual influence on Seattle's
Archbishop Raymond Hunthausen who himself
became a dedicated advocate of nuclear disarmament.

As activists, Jim and Shelley have for thirty years
been living martyrs to the power of non-violence:
standing firm against war; against the building and
possible deployment of nuclear weapons; against
military intervention in Iraq; and against racism, both
open and opaque. They lived for more than ten
years at "Ground Zero," just across the fence from
the naval station at Bangor, Washington, where the
first nuclear submarine was deployed. There they
witnessed, held seminars, and invited others to join
them. For ten years, Jim stood in the early morning
outside the gates at Bangor offering informational
leaflets to the workers building the most destructive
weapon the world has ever known. Jim loved those
workers, respected them totally, and won many,
including a Catholic chaplain at the base, to his point
of view. Jim also protested non-violently against the
coming of those first warheads, sitting on the tracks
to stop the "white train." Then, and many times
before and since, Jim was arrested.

What does Madalin have to do with all of this,
which is after all, her son's vocation?

Though I later got to know her well in other con-
texts, I saw Madalin initially and most frequently at
the daily Mass in our parish church. She was there
every day. Frequently Madalin would astound the

other worshippers, mostly elderly people like herself, with a prayer for her son.

"That my son will not be hurt as he sits on the railroad tracks to stop the train today, we pray to the Lord."

"For Jim and Shelley in the third week of their fast, that their health will not be hurt..."

"For my son in prison . . ."

"For my son, pleading for peace on the streets of Beirut (or Belfast, or Boston) . . ."

Almost every day Madalin prayed for her son in some dramatic situation.

She did so with both enormous pain at the suffering her son was taking on himself, yet with enormous pride in a son who stood against violence, against war, who *pitched his tent* alongside the victims of war and poverty all around the globe.

Jim was the son longing to convert a world to love, to usher in, as one of his books is titled, *The Coming of a Non-Violent God*. Jim was willing to undergo whatever violence came upon him as a result of living out his call; his non-violent convictions.

Madalin was the mother, the loving parent who stood by her son in his suffering, who watched in pain at the pain he suffered, but was so terribly proud of his willingness to do so. She agonized over his suffering, but rejoiced in his fidelity. She wept at his incarceration, but was thrilled by his courage. Madalin was never happy with Jim's suffering; it tore her up. But she understood the brokenness of our world and was so proud that Jim struggled to mend it. If this meant suffering for him, for her, so be it!

Madalin never explained all this, she simply lived it, while I and others watched, and learned, finally, something terribly important about God and his Christ, his Messiah.

We must be very careful how we speak the central truth of our faith. Jesus does not save us because he *suffers*, does not placate God because he *dies* a painful death. Jesus saves us because he is *faithful*, because he does not turn away from the suffering that love necessarily brings; does not stop loving, stop being non-violent, even if it leads to death.

God is not pleased because Jesus suffers. God is pleased because Jesus is obedient, faithful, courageous, and consistent "even unto death, even to death on a cross." Jesus learns obedience — learns the cost of being faithful — by the things that he suffers.

Maybe others can understand such notions in the abstract. Maybe others comprehend such truth by language alone. To begin to understand the mystery of God, I needed to see, mirrored in Madalin, this suffering love, this proud, painful support, this deep satisfaction in the faithfulness of her son, even while she hurt to her very bones with his pain.

I celebrate your life and death, Madalin Douglass, grateful for what you have taught me about our God.

My final words to you are the same as your final words to those who surrounded you at your death:

"Thank You."

Diana, Dee

Diana, Dee
Queen of the hunt,
Under moon's glow,
Seeking not game, but God,
Not food but future and hope,
Looking for love Gran gave,
Few since,
Hunting, as all are finally,
For what might mean
This messiness called "life."

Diana, Dee
Goddess of the moon,
Grateful,
finding, in herself, light,
When other's efforts dimmed,
Yet knowing herself not Sun,
No source,
But one illuminated.

Diana, Dee,
Pantheon Princess,
Inheriting prestige, power,
Position throughout the ages,
Now reduced to mortal state —
One of us,
Holding three jobs,
Dusting her own dirt,
Driving chariots
Heretofore long since demolished
Or offered to some servant.

Diana, Dee,
Husky and Harvard bred, brilliant,
Degreed and pedigreed,
Still, able to lose
Track of time,
Talents,
Things in her purse,
And her own needs.

Diana, Dee,
As reigning Goddess, giddy,
Smiling,
Sociable,
Able to move with grace
In myriad circles,
Veiling sadness, longing,
Hopes unfilled
Dreams dimmed
Or tarnished by time,
Awaiting Divine reward,
Her due.

Diana, Dee,
Bored by boards incessant,
But
Mother of a splendid Son,
Friend of the arts,
The mayor,
Car king,
Tennis pros and tennis bums,
Restaurateurs,
The Imprisoned
Or soon to be,
The needy child,
and, best of all,
Recently,
Me!

I celebrate
Your hunt,
Your find,
Your goddess stature,
If only in my eyes.

Entering into Marriage
"Never change horses in the middle of the stream . . ."
– Anonymous

Yet, in the middle of the stream
Great change.
Not a horse,
But more profound, precarious,
Even, one hopes, prayerful
Change.

Anonymous be damned!
Life's stream
Demands such new beginnings,
(The poet's been there).

To live
Insists on change,
On picking up the pieces,
Getting off the mat,
Returning to the ring,
Climbing on another horse
Or
Like Jesus,
Not staying on the ground
Embracing the fallen cross, but
Going farther up that deadly hill,
Hoping life lies beyond each big or little death.

To live
Insists we must
Say "Yes" again, . . .
Or, for the first time,
When the word
Stuck in our throat
Each time before.

To say "Forever"
With forever once so brief . . .
To say "I do,"
When I didn't,
Or haven't . . .
Courage incredible.

Young, promises are plentiful,
Having seen how easily these,
Like every other thing,
Break.
To pledge life-long love —
Is more like jumping off a bridge,
A speeding train,
or a horse that's run away.

As you embrace each other,
And the change life offers you,
Mid-stream or not,
I pray you both the Peace
That comes only to those who trust
A future not seen,
A hope not heard,
A heart never finally broken . . .
Who trust Love that conquers everything —

Trust Love. Not yours alone,
But God's for you,
As you begin today.

Memories of a Niece I Cherish
TallyAnn Turns Forty

These treasured few
From memories fond
Of forty years . . . a birthday gift.

A phone call
Unexpected,
Inviting me to lunch.
Worried through the menu to desert,
Waiting for the dropping of some crisis shoe.
None came,
Just your desire to spend time,
Amazingly,
with me.

Playing golf past dark
Before a simple meal shared.

Unnumbered family feasts,
Your trained thumb touching each
With love.

Your formal way with me,
Never simply "Pat,"
But "Father Carroll,"
Or now — a title I revere —
"Uncle."

Mostly, I recall,
Fragility,
Enduring almost endless pain,
Maintaining through each struggle
The warmest smile
God's earth has ever nurtured.

Divine Eyes
Never Close

Homeless

The city seldom sleeps,
Turning, tossing,
Oblivious of people
Crowded in single rooms,
Huddled on streets, near stairs against the wind,
    beneath bridges, or each other.

Divine eyes never close,
See the sleeper
And the sleepless blind,
And weep.

An Advent Prayer

A panic dwells within my heart tonight.
The future, like a cataract on eyes
Too ancient now to glimpse, too worldly wise
To trust your truth, brings only dreadful fright.

I cannot be what once I was, nor yet
Can see what possibilities arise
From ashes such as these; what hope from sighs
That wrack my nights. I'll pay my honest debt,
I'll speak the truth, so long held dormant in,
But, God, I seek some solace, beg some grace,
Cry out in longing for your once glimpsed face.

Still beating, blind, unpowered to begin,
My heart, despite a miracle of mend,
Shall cease unless some hope you send.

Blessed are They Who Mourn

"Oh Healing River . . . "
All Lent, we sang the waters down.
Prayed to wash, from sand, the blood
     Parched land to fertile valley,
Water to our lips,
     Our lives,
          Our loves.

Prayed baptism come,
Anew, for some,
Again, for all.

And then, today, at dawn . . .
Water — healing, living, Baptismal —
Tear-filled tub!

Tears of wars on, though victory vacuous,
    Of lives parched by pain,
    Of loves lost or lingering,
    From hunger,
        homelessness,
            hallucinations . . .

Our tears,
Human tears, abundant tears, healing tears,
Tears plunged into, buried into, dying into . . .

Into Easter!

Jesus born again —
    His amniotic fluid formed from tears;
    His tears, our tears.

Born (re-born) with Him,
We will cry again,
But we need never weep!

Christology from Below

It is not death that wins us, but the way
He lived — not the cross that saves us
But the powers he crossed, the lively fuss
Fomented in the courts of kings. To say,
"You fox," to Herod, or "hypocrite" to they
Who wore religious robes! To plant the seed
Of sanity in Sabbath's death, when need
Asked life. With humbled heart to boldly pray
And name their unimagined God his "Dad!"
Waste words with tarnished woman, and the meals
    he shared
With unregenerate men. These are the why
Of life for us, although he lived to die.
Had he loved otherwise would death still give
Breath bringing life to change the deaths we live?

No Comedy

The dreams the old man dreams concern what's gone;
The visions of the young with future rhyme
Their poem. But I, in muddled, middle-time
Am torn between. Not young, to carry on
My hope to ever be a bit of all my youth
Had seen, when naïve visions prompted zest,
Nor old enough to have to be at rest
With what, preceding now, must mask as truth.

So, somewhat Dante-like, I wander, caught between
The heaven sighted, but not sealed, and hell,
Whose counterpart, known so well
(For certainly, I've every circle seen.)

This purging time, I tarry . . . perhaps pray,
No vision, dream, nor Beatrice to show the way.

Goodbyes Make
My Throat Hurt

I came to tell a story
which you have told to me;
the story of Jesus.
This story will never end,
nor will our bonded love,
our lives, our laughter
ever never be.

Now,
as Charlie Brown to Snoopy,
so I to you,
with lumped throat,
say,
"Farewell."

But Christians never say "goodbye,"
Only, "So long. I'll see you."

Doubtless
(even in this fragile life)
our crosses will path again.

We will meet here,
hereafter,
and forever.

Love never ends.

Incarnation

Flesh, like ours,
Skin, bones, bowels,
Heart that can break, bleed, wear out,
Eyes to cry, see, see through, grow dim,
Tongue to taste, savor, speak, lash,
Touching, building, breaking, holding hands,
Ears hearing words, winds, wisdom, warnings —
In everything, like us.
Whatever God might be,
not distant now, but near,
Among.

On this creed, tenuous,
Hangs my fragile hope.

Lesotho

"Wherever You Are, You Bring Yourself With You."

Rugged land of cragged, jagged buttes,
Greened now by storms, relentless rains,
Its omnipresent mountains, wordy mutes
That speak of heaven grasped at, from the pains
Of people underneath them, who, peaceful, wait
Their kind of hell, who number loss and gains
By different standards in their laughing state
Enjoy expectant pace, peculiar, slow,
No measured out by spoons of hate.

An ageless, timeless, patient people know
They'll wait perhaps a little longer still
For unpromised blessings — a winter's snow,
Providing spring-time waters from a hill
Behind their hut — a day when they can dwell in
   houses made of brick not dung — when feast
   they will
Like collared Europeans — when birth bell
That ushers life implies they will endure.
And, while they wait, they laugh at time, at hell,
At everything, and sing melodious harmonies, so sure
In many parts, to God imposed by others,
But, now, their own, and loved . . . so simple, pure.

I see them from behind my constant glass,
My windows, separate, psychological and real.
Beyond my reach, they sign, they laugh, they pass
Apart, by language, culture, or, perhaps, the feel
Of my insecurity. But with a passion fond
I love them all, untouched. I kneel
Before their most articulate bond
Of silent accusation, and their disturbing call
To come, drink deeply, from their wisdom's pond.

To live with less inquiry of "why,"
Simple, poor, unprided in the things I own,
Complete for now with no demanding ties.
Happy just with being, and able so to be, alone,
To struggle with the elements outside,
And inner emptiness without a moan.
Strong, aging like thin trees, with pride,
Carefully amid the whirling winds of chance
Sweeping over and around, most often wide,
But rarely through their lives, they dance
To me the folly of my holding tightly
On to life, or any part. Their stance
Is free, and so must it ever be, for rightly
Do they know that all, all will pass away —
A wisdom at the core of life seen brightly
By those who must find life there every day.

Thus, traveling far away, I bring my "I,"
Everything I see or hear has much to say,
The storm, the constant God-voiced cry
Pounds at my deafened heart; the, like me,
Insistent mountains do not lie —
The people's poverty, a challenging to be
So much less needy
   in my dreams
   and hopes,
What's outside,
   different,
   familiar
   becomes; I see
Myself against
   Lesotho's lovely
   slopes.

Beatitude

Marvelous old man,
Basotho, bowed, steady smiling
Taught true that Gospel line
Read so smugly Sunday morning.

Surely no mistake of mine
Explained my money, visas, passport
Passed away, and dead to me.
So many pitied me my loss;
I relished their concern,
If not the thingy death that gave it rise.
So richly I deserved their care —
Too easily blamed the place,
The people, anyone or thing but me —
Wept tears of one unjustly hurt,
Moaning mistaken manner of my loss.

Then, he stood,
Reached beneath his battered blanket,
Bowed his softly smiling head,
Handed what was lost, now found,
Then turned to go away,
Rewarded by his own accustomed honesty.

A humbled sufferer,
I handed him a paltry part
Of that which he could so easily
Have taken all.
He turned again away —
Expecting nothing
Of the all he'd found,
Yet needing much, much more.
His thanks to me,
That strange, still steady smile
The Lord had promised him
(Though he, perhaps, had never heard
This Jesus-pledge, he knew it deeply in his bones,
From years of honest, joy-rewarded
Toil and trial.)
The smile, etched deep in ancient lines,
Broadened none at his expected act
That lit my face with undeserved relief.

As he enfleshed, "The poor are blessed,"
I pray he taught me more
Than merely "sorrowing can be consoled"
(Some sorrows scarcely so deserve),
That humbled by his happiness,
I can perhaps begin that earth to gain
With which that poor but honest man
Is One!

Stormed Memory

Over a land so parched, so rudely slashed
By winter's dryness, ceaselessly downpours
Light's darkest storm. Unnerving, calling roars
Of thunder. Momentary lightening flashed,
Idea'd his whole horizon with a light
Belying numbness, dumbness, storm instilled.
Divine, demanding voice away, he willed,
But knocks it constant on his tin roof's night.

Now, only light reminding rain remains
Without. Within, unwinds a mystery
Unveiled by the storm, some history
Forgotten now, beneath the wind, the rains,
But wrenching to revive, grown sadly dim,
The night that awesome power stormed at him!

To A Contemplative
Anglican Sister

Distracted active priest of Roman bent,
Quiet, cloistered sisters of that English branch:
Strange meeting!
To teach a language spoken haltingly
To those most fluent, affluent,
Where he is poor indeed.

Does frequent eating cause a hunger
One turns anywhere to fill?
Does inconstant nibbling create
Confidence to give one's bit away?

To Newcastle, a single lump of coal,
An ice cube to a smiling Eskimo,
This single talent is invested too.

How graciously the wise adult
Receives the open offering of a child!

Surprise

They meet,
And even though I am not there,
I leap, I laugh, I celebrate,
Perhaps the greatest joy
We joy-filled humans touch.

To have our friends be friends,
The ones we love, each other love.
Whatever flows from such a grace
Is theirs,
Yet always, also, mine.

My sister, African,
My second mother,
        (San Franciscan)
Parts precious of my life
Joined.
Me, there, however distant.
I, again, am one,
As Jesus prayed —
The world can believe.

My God, I swear,
There is no greater human unity
In this so shaky world —
Or the next (rumored to be permanent) —
That meeting one here,
Another there,
And know that meeting
(Too chance to happen otherwise)
Flows from the overflow of Love
That I've been gifted with,
And cannot but be thrilled
To share.

No Branch Grows Alone
(John 15)

The vine entwines all branches one,
The branches sense.
Still long they for a union, each with each,
Out-reaching Super-Nature's own.
No chance! Some say, "No need."
But want, oh want, indeed.

A single gracing rain instills what life
These branches have.
Who'd search for other rain, new source
Besides the vine's already joining life?
No search, but still, somehow is found
New soil, and sweet, fresh ground.

Each growing branch reaches for strength
Believed beyond the Vine's —
For strength that other, tender branches give,
Believing briefly, wrongly, this strength is self-possessed.

It is the Vine's, The Vine's alone!
Now shared—new known!

Life's Labor Lost

Tears,
large, humongous tears,
tears stored up,
        through years unwept,
Flowing out onto a
        (till now)
Barren ground.

I have loved my life, till now,
        and now,
I've lost it,
        squandered really.

No longer will I speak aloud
A word I've heard from You,
No longer raise my voice
Aloud,
In public prayer to You,
For us.

Broken,
even if raised up
I will — amid these tears —
be mute about it.

Tears flow and will not stop.

Tears too,
because an image of myself
     has died,
And falls on barren ground.

The face my mirror saw
These sixty years
Was smiling.
Now it weeps,
tears,
     humongous tears,
     on barren ground.

I am not what I told myself I was,
and cannot yet put trust
in one I may become.

These tears meanwhile
tear at my heart,
my spirit,
for what I've lost,
        squandered really.

Tears flowing
on ground
        too barren yet
        to let the liquid in
so life can grow
        out of some new
        and watered garden.
Watered with these tears
Until it blooms with life,
This (till now)
Barren ground.

On Taking Leave
of the Life I've Known

I've known "shock" before. My heart depends
On it. Still, this new shock shakes all I know,
Uproots all understanding, tragic ends
All I till now surmised. In truth, trust though
In God endures, but shaken, stirred, disturbed
Beyond cognition. How be Love
Revealed beneath a host of deeply perturbed
Companions? How through this muddled move
Will grace appear? How being priest no more,
Brother no more, may in some scheme of things
Be best, how somehow touch the very core
Of truth, to offer broken Spirit wings?

Although I cannot now see how this come
I wait in prayerful darkness, muted, dumb.

Who Am I Now?

All these years
of knowing who I am
by how I signed myself.
How strange that space
there, after my name,
blank, bland, empty.

At first we signed it little, n.s.j.
Novices, beginners, small case.

How proud to put S.J. there
after all those L's,
Telling the world to whom it was that
I belonged.
Books by *me*, S.J.
articles by *me*, S.J.
Countless letters
to editors, friends, enemies,
and other companions,
telling what I believed,
what I was about,
not just by text,
but how I signed myself
proudly, easily,
lazily,
sometimes dishonestly.
Society of Jesus

I stare at my name today
and wonder
as I will in days ahead,
Who I am,
and will become.
To whom can I belong,
what company, companionship, society
if not Jesus?
I just can't tell the world — each time,
can't remind myself — each time,
It has to be inside,
as all along
I've wanted to be
Society of Jesus.

No Words

Sixty-two miraculous years,
Forty-four as Jesuit,
Thirty-one as priest,
all as fragile,
holding back the storm.

Appearing to some as rock,
firm against the waves;
known to others, close,
as sand.

Articulate, wise, witty,
even arrogant,
but, under, stuttering.

Warm, yet alone,
Competent, untrained,
Despite polio,
    apparently unparalyzed,
Health's picture,
    with a heart machine,
belonging, while estranged.
Always wondering
when the shoe would drop,
the tide go out,
and all discover
that I'm swimming naked.

It did,
I am.

The Christ-Cross,
(All I've ever truly trusted)
alone remains.

I await
in awful
unaccustomed silence,
promised
Resurrection.

Ready and Willing

Thought I was . . .

Three decades plus prove
Beneath the whipped cream,
Less than chocolate.

Willingly, and well
I did the tasks —
Proclaimed a Wisdom Word
Not my own —
With requisite awe
Presided over Mystery,
Stood by graves
With honest tears —
By couples' covenants
With honest hope —
With compassion unfeigned
Felt with sinners sorrow,
All easily,
Acknowledging
Death and hope and failure
In myself.

Somewhere I recall
A cinematic shrink maintained,
"Get the gestures right,
The motives will follow."
Not true!

I always had the gestures,
Words and ways,
But missed the motives;
Why and *how* escaped me.

Despite Faith's deepening,
Divine intimacy left unfilled,
Heart given;
Flesh refused to follow.

Longing to link
        Love-Incarnate
        With fragile fellowship
        Self stayed central
        Revealing sometimes God
Too often only brokenness.

I can no more
Be priest,
The flesh too raw
Cost too dear,
Heart's hope fallen
Like its wounded vessel
Un-defibrillated.

Willing,
But no longer,
Perhaps not ever,
Ready.

Is anybody ever?

Reluctant Surrender
My Suscipe

Suicide
Is done
Not
Deciding death
But rather wanting
Not to live this way.

Deed unimaginable
Sense the same.

I do not choose
The half-life,
Shelved.

Heart attacked
Inside and out,
No energy to live,
No life left anyway.

I long for Death
(better, being Dead).

I do not choose.

My choice?
Something different, something else,
Something?

My choice?
To have the past present
Heart, health, name,
Whole.

My choice?
Living, loving, leaving
The wounds behind.

My choice?
A cross made of wood,
Not would, could, should.

Still,
My best choices led me
To this choiceless moment.

You,
Finally,
Win.

Sex

It's always a metaphor.

Something in itself, surely,
But image too, beyond the act —
even messier.

Impotence, admit,
Not merely sexual,
But human, genderless, universal,
Part or all
Of everyone.
Who does not know oneself as
Powerless,
Limp,
Early ripe, early rotten,
Promising more than ever is delivered?
"Never up, never in," golf pros,
Sexologists, psychologists,
Poets, all agree.

We want to give
So much more than we have,
Want to share,
More than we possess,
Want to pour ourselves like geysers
Into the waiting other,
But almost always fail,
Leaving both
Disappointed, waiting still
For more.

So easily, initially excited,
We fail the follow through,
Can't stay alert waiting till the master comes
(It's always a metaphor).
We fall asleep unspent,
Spirit willing, flesh weak
(It's always a metaphor).

A human poverty beneath,
Deeper, than body
or Body part,
The very heart and hurt of who we are,
Not Potent,
Never enough,
Not God!

Silent

Celebrating a Child's Death

Silent,
too frequently,
I stood,
Years past,
As priest,
Heart wrenched
by child's death.

Too often,
Knowing parents' pain,
Or friends' frustration,
longing to support the insupportable —
Ancient ache,
A broken world's disorder.

Silent,
Called, somehow, to *celebrate*.
Searching for Spirit words
To speak aloud,
Effing the ineffable;
Silent,
Wondering
If even an apparently
Infinite God
(Presuming truth that
more than ever
cried for proof)
Could now speak,
Could tell us, clearly,
Why?

Knowing I could not.

Before me
Broken hearts,
Parched lands,
Hopeless deserts,
Thirsting for waters
Beyond my witching wand
Of words.

Finally,
I spoke.
One must.

Spoke to family numb,
Fragile friends,
Mostly to my muted self.
Spoke poetry not mine,
Syllables, images, metaphors
From that unconscious place
Of *Faith*,
deeply darkened,
Hope
Battered, clung to,
Love,
beyond any articulate
reason.

Order Form

Use the form below to order additional autographed copies of *A Crooked Finger Beckons*. Make checks payable to Consigning Women, call in or mail your charge card information. Please call us for any questions or email: consigningwomen1@earthlink.net

Name _____

Address _____

City _____ State _____ Zip _____

Phone _____

Please send me _____ books at $17.95 each $_____

Tax = .088 (Washington State Residents) $1.58 each $_____

Postage and package: $5.95 each $_____

Total enclosed $_____

Mastercard, Visa_____ Exp. Date _____
(We take American Express orders over the phone, also.)

Mail to:
Consigning Women, LLC
2460 Canterbury Lane East, Number 5A
Seattle, Washington 98112
(206) 861-8112